Stories For Me

By Anita Cheríe

Stories For Me by Anita Cherìe

Copyright © 2024 by Anita Cherìe

All rights reserved. Published by

Blue Café Books *for*
www.carladupont.com
Atlanta, GA

Printed in the USA.

ISBN: 979-8-218-39129-4

Credits
Editorial: Carla DuPont
Cover Design: Garrett Myers

DEDICATION

This book is dedicated to every student who desires to become a better reader. It is specifically dedicated to middle school students who feel like they are struggling daily to comprehend reading material in all of their core classes. It is written for students who struggle to read and comprehend the information necessary to independently complete their classroom assignments.

NOTE TO STUDENTS

The only way to become a better reader is to read. Remember to start with the basics and challenge yourself to get a little stronger everyday. Determine your strongest reading level and celebrate your success when you clearly understand what you are reading. Begin reading as many books as you can at that level. Then keep going.

You can do this! Let's start here.

CONTENTS

Begin 1

Believe...6

Next 14

Then 19

Finally 26

Stories For Me
By Anita Cheríe

A big blue ball is in the box.
I can run and jump.
Can you help me find the cat?
Go away.

Where are you?
Here I am.

Do you see a yellow cat?

I see two cats.
I am funny.
I see one cat.
It is not funny.
Look for the red box.
Look for the blue ball in the red
box.

I see three cats.
My box is not red.

I see the little one in the box.
Can you see it?
I can see it.
Can you see it?
I said I can see it!

I can make a funny face.
We can run and play.
I can jump up and down.
Come down to the car.

BELIEVE

I am smart.
I am funny.
Let me tell you what I did.

I had a bag of chips.
I ate all the chips.
The black cat came to see me.
I did not give him any chips.
I just looked at him.

How are you?
You must be mad.
I am not mad.
I am good.
I am on my way out.

Our cat is pretty.
He is so soft.
They will play with him.

I went to the park.
Now I want to ride my bike.
I saw a girl at the park.
I said, "I will be here all day."
She did not say hello to me.
I left the park.

Are you at the park?
I will be back soon.

I will sit in the brown car.
I will eat this food.
It is in the bag.

I played a game as soon as I
got home.

There was a big dog in the
yard. He wanted to play a
game too.

That was fun for me.

I looked under the bed.
What did I see?
I saw a white sock.
Who put this sock under the
bed?

I said," I will eat the chips" but
the dog wants the chips.
I said no.
Please get this dog.
He is in the box.
I will jump into the box.
I have a new white hat.
It is pretty.
I want it but it is too big.

We ran fast.
Now we are on our way to the park.
Can I ride with you?

I got into the car.
I went to the store.
Now I have a new hat.
I like my new hat.

I do not feel well.
I will sit down.
Will you sit with me?
Yes, I will sit with you.

Do you have four quarters?
I do.
I will get them for you.
You are so good to me.

Can we go again?
I will go after my nap.
I do not have any money.
I have an apple.

Pat is going to see her son.
She got a tag from the man.
She can fly.

Put the old box on top of the
blue box.
It is just a box.
It may be too big.
I will give you every ball in this
box.

This is how you open the box.

The man had a round ball.
Sam has the ball.

I have to make it stop.
Then I will open the door.

Do you know where to go?
She will ask them.
She told me once.
I think I will ask her again.
Can we go over there?
We could try.

Where were you?
I am here.
When did you see her?
I saw her yesterday.
I want some of the cans.
Do not take them to her.

I had to say Thank You.

The cat will live under the
brown box.
I will give it to you.
I will walk as fast as I can.
I will walk by the cat.

When will we walk?
We will walk the dog after he
eats.

His dog is big.
I will help him with his dog.

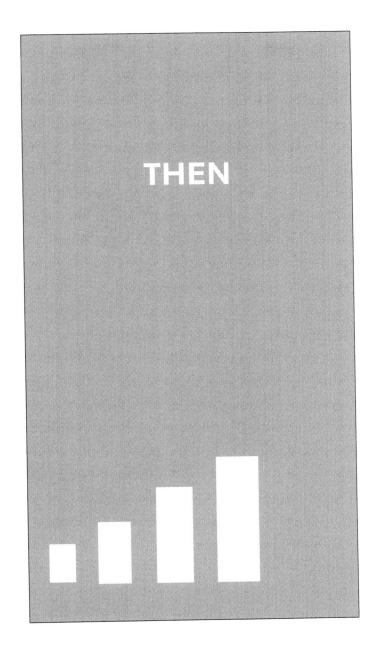

I always have a plan.
I had to turn around because I left my bag.
This is the best way to go.

Which one do you want?
I want both of the bags.
I will buy them.

I don't know how to help you.

Does she know how to help me?

Will you call her now or later?

Where have you been?
I have a cold.
I will call you before I come
over.

The car is fast.
My dad gave it to me.
He found it in the box.
How many cars did he find?
He found five cars.
I have the green car.

I was the first one to go to bed. She goes to bed after I go to bed.

I made a big bag of popcorn. I will sleep in my bed.

I can read. I can write.

Once upon a time I saw a little pig. The pig was in its pen.

Why did you step over the pig?

There were so many blue
boxes on the mat.
Can you pull these for us?

Did you get a red hat or a blue
hat?

These are their hats.
Tell them to come get their
hats.

Those are mine.
Take them off.

I use the big blue mat.
It is very soft.
I will wash it now.
Will you go with us?
We will sit down.
I will sit on your mat with you.

I will go with you right now.
We will sing a song.
I wish you had a big mat.
We would sit together.
We would work on our math.

Anita Cherìe

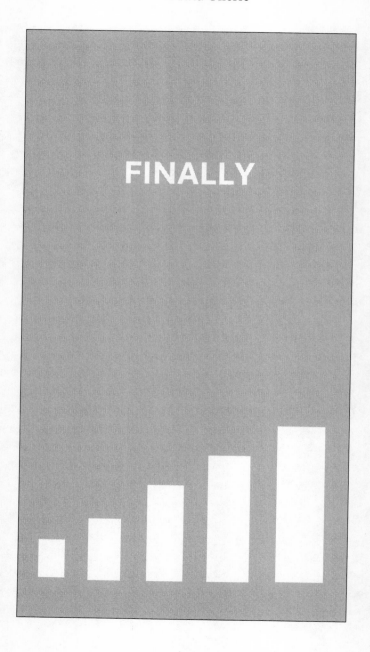

I have too much to do today.
We can work together.
She is so kind.

That hat is too small.
How much does that hat cost?
I will give you ten dollars for
that hat.
There are seven hats in the
box.
I only have six dollars.
She will never say that again.

Let's talk about the show.
I want to pick a new show to
watch on TV.
I have eight boxes.
This is the only box for you.
I want you to try this food.

I have a long stick.
I like to draw.
I will draw a picture of a cat
and a dog.
I am proud of myself.

Are you done with your cup?
My cup is full.
Will you bring me the cup?
I have my own mug.
I will keep it warm for you.
I will make it better for you.

I have a new blue mat.
I will clean the mat
I will cut the tag.
I sat my drink on the mat.

I will not run fast.
I do not want to fall.
I will run far.

I got a new bag.
The little bag was light.
Give it to me.
I will keep it for you.

The pot was hot.
I hurt my hand.
Will you hold my hand?
I feel better.
Please don't worry about me.
Shall we dance?

The plant will grow.
It will take about five weeks.
I will wait.
I will laugh if the joke is funny.

I am proud of you.

34827715R00024